The Little Book of Maths Outdoors

by Terry Gould
Illustrations by Mike Phillips

LITTLE BOOKS WITH BIG IDEAS

Published 2011 by A&C Black, Bloomsbury Publishing plc
50 Bedford Square, London, WC1B 3DP
www.acblack.com

ISBN 978-1-4081-4560-9

Text © Terry Gould
Illustrations © Mike Phillips

A CIP record for this publication is available from the British Library.
All rights reserved. No part of this publication may be reproduced
in any form or by any means – graphic, electronic, or mechanical, including
photocopying, recording, taping or information storage or retrieval systems –
without the prior permission in writing of the publishers.

Printed in Great Britain by Latimer Trend & Company Limited

This book is produced using paper that is made from wood grown in
managed, sustainable forests. It is natural, renewable and recyclable.
The logging and manufacturing processes conform to the environmental
regulations of the country of origin.

**To see our full range of titles
visit www.acblack.com**

Contents

Introduction

The Little Book of Maths Outdoors provides a range of tried, tested and motivational mathematical based outdoor activities. These aim to support young children's mathematical development through concrete, active, hands-on experiences. Alongside developing children's mathematics skills, the activities will help to develop their communication and thinking skills, physical skills and social and emotional development. In this way this book is very much in line with the recently published EYFS review recommendation (April 2011).

Proposed reforms to the EYFS framework

Dame Clare Tickell's EYFS review (April 2011) recommended a focus on three prime areas - personal, social and emotional development; communication and language; and physical development. Her review also recommended that within these areas there should be an emphasis on developing literacy, MATHEMATICS, expressive arts and design and understanding the world. Using the ideas in this book will ensure that your setting is prepared and able to introduce some of these changes, while remaining up-to-date with further developments.

Mathematics for young children is about children:

- ▶ seeking patterns and making connections
- ▶ recognising relationships between numbers, shapes and quantities
- ▶ using their knowledge and skills to solve problems
- ▶ generating new questions and making connections across other areas of learning and development.

(Children Thinking Mathematically 2009)

All the activities in this book can be linked to the prime areas of:

Personal, Social and Emotional Development

Children are encouraged to talk about ideas, select resources and say when they need help. Making relationships is part of this prime area, as is working cooperatively in a group, taking turns and helping each other.

Physical Development

Children experience handling a range and variety of resources and equipment as they engage in this type of play. Given the nature of using familiar everyday resources and materials, and being outside, children will also learn about safety issues.

Communication and Language

Speaking, listening and expressing their thinking will naturally arise because of the nature of these practical activities in the outside environment. As children engage in and see the outcomes of their play, they will be thinking about how best to succeed in the games. Part of this process will be raising questions and trying to provide answers.

The importance of outdoor learning

The ongoing provision of high quality outdoor learning is an entitlement for all children in the Early Years and will continue to be an important requirement of the new Early Years framework. Practitioners should provide opportunities for all children to engage in learning through play and hands-on activity – promoted through both adult-led and child-initiated learning.

This must include mathematical learning and development in the aspects of:

▶ Numbers and Calculating

▶ Shape, Space and Measures

Outdoors is where many young children really want to be. Being outdoors can offer them more opportunities to engage in a whole range of activities on a bigger scale and without worrying about levels of noise, mess made or having enough space. Outdoor learning can have a really positive impact on children's well being and development. They can access the fresh air and space and move in much faster and more complex ways. Some children are also likely to learn more effectively outdoors – particularly those with a more kinaesthetic learning style – often this is the boys, but many of the girls too!

The activities in this book use a range of low cost and easily available natural and household resources rather than those, often of greater expense, which practitioners are often tempted to buy from glossy educational catalogues because they are titled as 'educational'. They include such things as cardboard boxes, guttering, string, and jumbo chalk.

Visualisation and maths as fun

Recent guidance stresses the importance of visualisation in developing young children's mathematical concepts, including the use of number lines and tracks in outdoor mathematical learning. This key message and others are incorporated into all the activities.

Young children can and should experience mathematical ideas as a fun and exciting part of the process of exploring, finding out and making sense of the world they live in. The perception of being no good at mathematics usually starts early on, when children are thrust into the use of abstract symbols before they have a secure understanding of underlying concepts. One of the most important ideas that practitioners in the early years can take on board is the importance of visualisation for children and the need for them to engage with concrete experiences to secure conceptual understanding before moving on to the abstract.

Children writing numbers are best supported by:

▶ Practitioners who show interest in the marks they make

▶ Settings which provide a wide range of resources and materials to write numbers with, both indoors and outdoors

▶ Practitioners who model writing numbers

▶ Practitioners who set up games and activities where children are motivated to explore and write numbers

Significantly, it is recognised that Mathematical vocabulary needs to be set in purposeful contexts and not taught out of context or as a list to be remembered.

(Children Thinking Mathematically, DCSF 2009/Numbers And Patterns, DCSF 2010)

Motivating children

Motivating children to be excited about their learning is of the highest importance in developing a positive climate for learning. Ausubel (Educational Psychology, a cognitive view, 1968) has suggested that there are three factors which support motivation to be involved and undertake a task:

▶ Interest in the task

▶ The effect the task has on our image of ourselves

▶ Whether the task accords us links with other people

Whilst my own personal experiences have shown me that young children are motivated by:

▶ Success

▶ Enjoyment

▶ Appropriate challenge

Significantly, the activities in this book are motivating for children because of all the above factors, but equally important is the fact that they take place outdoors; which in many cases is where young children want to be.

The role of the practitioner

The importance of the practitioner modelling the activity and supporting and encouraging children to participate can't be understated. However, the longer term ideal is that children begin to engage independently with the activities and that they can access the resources and materials as part of the continuous outdoor provision on offer. The role of the adult is to accord this type of outdoor maths activity a high status and help the children to engage independently with the resources, sometimes creating their own 'changed' or modified rules. Critically, children are not under pressure in these activities to get the right answer, and mathematics is made inviting to them. As a result, a positive disposition towards mathematics can be developed from early on and learning and development outcomes are often much improved.

Settings which have trialled the activities in this book have found they made significant gains in all areas, but most significantly in the area of 'Calculating' (this includes Medlock Primary School, in inner city Manchester). Practitioners are also required, and need, to develop parental partnerships and understanding of the purpose and value of mathematical experiences. As many of these activities can also be undertaken in the home environment, they can be effectively used to support and develop this shared understanding.

Summary

Practitioners should ensure that:

▶ every day is potentially a 'Mathematics Day' (outdoors and indoors)

▶ mathematics is made fun, active, and interesting

▶ hands-on, active outdoor learning is seen as important both to practitioners and parents

▶ we support 'talking mathematics' that clarifies and refines children's thinking

▶ children are enabled to visualise mathematics through models, resources and images that support their learning.

Balls and boxes

This is an ideal game to set up as a targeted activity where the practitioner spends a short time only at the activity and children engage independently for most of the time.

Ideas for focus:

▶ To be able to count on and add together small numbers using an outdoor number line

▶ To problem solve in order to work out the best strategies to obtain the highest score

▶ To record the outcomes of the activity

What you need:

▶ 2–5 medium-sized cardboard boxes (crisp boxes are ideal)

▶ a piece of guttering (approx 1 metre long)

▶ a variety and range of small and medium-sized balls

▶ jumbo chalk

▶ a chalkboard

▶ 1–2 milk crates (or similar sized boxes)

▶ a bucket for the balls

▶ an outdoor number line

Key mathematical language:

bigger, smaller, heavier, lighter, how many, more than, less than, nearer, further away

Before you start:

▶ Cut two holes into each of your cardboard boxes (for the balls to roll into). Chalk or otherwise fix numbers above the holes. Ideally start with numbers 1 and 2 only, adding higher numbers as the children gain more skills

▶ Chalk a straight line. Place 2–5 cardboard boxes behind the chalked line.

▶ Chalk a start line where the end of the guttering will be when rolling the balls down it and write the word 'START'. Use a milk crate (or box) to sit the guttering on, although, as they become more proficient at this game, children can hold and direct the the guttering themselves.

▶ Supply a variety of balls in a trug or bucket for children to choose from.

▶ Hang the chalkboard from a nearby fence or wall or use a freestanding easel.

What you do:

1. Explain how to play the game: each child has two turns to roll a ball down the guttering and into one of the numbered holes. When a ball rolls into a hole, the child scores the number that is written above that hole. Once the child has had two goes, the numbers are added together to make the final score, so for example, if the first ball rolled goes into the hole marked 1 and the second ball rolled goes into the hole marked 2, the total score would be 3. Explain the rules repeatedly as required.

2. Now, demonstrate the game to the children. Demonstrate with a variety of different balls. Give the children time to practise rolling the balls down the guttering and into the holes in the boxes before starting for real!

And another idea:

▶ Have three different starting lines where children can move up a challenge level by starting from a little further back.

▶ Add more varieties or sizes of balls.

▶ Change the size and shape of the holes.

▶ Provide the resources in easily accessible ways for children to self-select and set up in their free choice periods.

Cars on the run

This is an ideal game to set up as a targeted activity where the practitioner spends a short time only at the activity and children engage independently for most of the time.

Ideas for focus:

▶ To predict distances

▶ To score using a 1st, 2nd and 3rd basis

▶ To add small numbers together using an outdoor number line

What you need:

▶ a range of different sizes and types of toy car

▶ a piece of guttering (approximately 1m long) with a flat bottom

▶ 2 milk crates or similar sized boxes

▶ jumbo chalk and pencils

▶ a chalkboard (to record on)

▶ small white plastic seed/plant markers

▶ an outdoor number line and clothes pegs

Key mathematical language:

fast, slow, higher, lower, nearest, bigger, smaller, 1st, 2nd, 3rd, number names

Before you start:

▶ Chalk a start line where the end of the guttering will be when the toy cars are rolled down it and write the word 'START' alongside it. Use a milk crate or box to sit the guttering on (although, as the children become more proficient at this game, they can hold and direct the guttering themselves).

▶ Chalk ten lines equidistance apart and in parallel to the start line (ideally 80–100mm apart), numbering them in order from 1–10.

▶ Supply the variety of cars in a box for children to choose from.

▶ Hang the chalkboard from a nearby fence or wall or use a freestanding easel.

What you do:

1. Allow children time to look at the toy cars and practise rolling them down the guttering.

2. Explain how to play the game: each child selects a car and predicts where it will stop on the chalk 'road' by placing a plant marker on the 'road'. Then they roll their car down the guttering and see how close their prediction was!

3. Ask each player to write their name on a plant marker in pencil.

4. Demonstrate predicting and placing the plant marker where they think the car will stop, and then rolling the car down the guttering and comparing where the car actually stopped with where they placed their marker. Demonstrate this as many times as is required for everyone to understand.

5. Now encourage the children to 'predict and roll'.

6. Explain how the scoring will work: the child whose car stops closest to their plant marker will score 3 points, the next closest will score 2 points and the next closest will score 1 point. Decide how many turns each child will have – it is good to start with two turns. After two turns the winner is the child with the highest score, i.e. the child who made the closest/most accurate predictions.

7. Have a practice run to ensure everyone understands how to play the game and how the scoring works.

8. Work with children in small groups as an adult guided activity.

9. When adding up the scores, model how to use the number line with pegs.

And another idea:

▶ Consider raising the height of the guttering by adding a second crate. Explore what difference this makes – most children predict it will make the car go further.

Swap circle

Ideas for focus:

▶ To recognise and name numbers up to and beyond 10

▶ To listen and respond to simple instructions with a mathematical focus

What you need:

▶ jumbo chalk to draw the circle or a ready marked/painted surface

▶ number cards up to the required numbers in the circle

▶ a hat (for the person who is taking the turn of the caller)

▶ a two minute sand or wind-up timer

Key mathematical language:

number names, one more, one less

Before you start:

▶ Draw a circle with numbers marked on it using jumbo chalk, children's paint or use an existing painted circle. Use numbers that are appropriate to the children's developmental stage.

What you do:

1. Invite the children to stand in a circle, each child standing beside a number (so that they can still see the number).

2. Put on the 'caller' hat and ask the children to change places by calling out instructions e.g. 'Whoever is standing on number 3 swap places with the person standing on number 5!' You might want to demonstrate this first with one of the more confident children.

3. Display number cards to reinforce the name and shape of the numbers being referred to.

4. Continue calling out pairs of numbers until everyone has had a turn of swapping places or the two minute timer has gone.

And another idea:

▶ Let a child wear the 'caller' hat and take the role of number caller. The adult should support the child initially, then step back once the child is confident to call out the numbers independently. Use the timer and when the time is up another child could take the role of caller.

▶ When asking children to swap use more challenging language, e.g, 'The person who is standing on the number that is 1 more than 7 swap with the person standing on 1 less than 3'.

Dress the tree

Ideas for focus:

▶ To create a range and variety of patterns

What you need:

▶ a small fir tree planted in a suitable spot outdoors (or alternatively an artificial tree set into a bucket of concrete)

▶ a variety and range of safe and non breakable tree decorations (need to risk assess) including things like baubles, tinsel, garlands, other hanging decorations

▶ a child-friendly digital camera

Key mathematical language:

smaller, larger, round, long, short, on top, underneath, next to, behind

Before you start:

▶ Ensure that the range of Christmas tree decorations are safe for children to use and are sorted into boxes for easy access.

What you do:

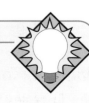

1. Model decorating the tree to create and recreate patterns by choosing and putting items onto the tree e.g, garlands, baubles, crackers, etc. Point out where they might place the items and consider showing them a picture of a decorated tree. Do the children recognise that the patterns are created by the way the objects are placed? Do they recognise that they are making an irregular pattern and every time the tree is dressed it will be a different pattern?

2. Show the children the digital camera and how to record the patterns created with the tree decorations.

3. Work with the children in small groups as a focused/adult guided activity

4. Remind the children that they decide where to place the objects on the tree and they don't have to use every item available.

And another idea:

▶ Support the children to engage in free play, working cooperatively to record the patterns made with the tree decorations by using the camera or drawing sketches.

▶ Encourage the children to make books of their tree patterns, with comments.

Crate maze

Use as a focused led activity for 4–6 children working individually.

Ideas for focus:

▶ To engage the children in problem solving strategies

▶ To add scores together to get larger numbers (size of numbers to be differentiated by the stage of the children's development)

What you need:

▶ 2–3 milk crates

▶ several A4 sized rectangular trays

▶ A4 sized paper or card

▶ collections of objects such as bottle tops (red, green and blue), small pebbles, draughts', not counters

▶ a wall or fence-mounted board or handheld clipboards (to mark scores on)

▶ marker pens

▶ string

▶ a washing line with numbers pegged on it (number line)

Key mathematical language:

through, bottom, top, number names, colour names, round

Before you start:

▶ Using string, fasten the milk crates to the fence (or wall) with the top of the crates towards the fence and the bottom of the crate facing forwards. Ensure that the crates are at a suitable height so that the children are able to easily reach up to drop objects through the crate from the top.

▶ Place the trays in a row underneath the crates, with A4 paper or card attached to the inside bottom with a number written on it. This will be the score if an object lands in the tray. Start off with 1, 2, 3, moving to higher numbers as the children become more experienced and develop their number and calculating skills.

▶ Display the number line.

What you do:

1. Explain how to play the game: each child takes a turn to drop an object into the top of the crate with the aim of it cascading through the crate and eventually landing in one of the trays underneath. Each child will have a specific number of objects, e.g. 2 or 3. The child will score the number written on the tray that the object lands in. Once the child has taken their 2–3 turns, their scores are added up to make a total.

2. Allow the children time to experiment – dropping different objects through the crates.

3. Help the children to use the number line to add their scores up.

And another idea:

▶ Allow the children to take control of the activity, including deciding on any changes to the rules, types of objects to be used and numbers on the trays.

Shape statues

This is an ideal activity for a larger group of children.

Ideas for focus:

▶ To listen carefully and follow instructions

▶ Think about and verbalise the properties of shapes

What you need:

▶ a suitable hard surface e.g. tarmac

▶ jumbo chalk

▶ a musical instrument, such as a drum, or CD recorded music and a music player

Key mathematical language:

names of standard shapes, properties of shapes: wavy edge, straight edges, circular edge, thin, narrow, wide, long

Before you start:

▶ Ideally, use the space that you use in your setting for ball games/running activities.

What you do:

1. Explain the rules to the children and what they need to do: when the music stops they have to make themselves into a statue shape.

2. The adult can describe the shape in simple language for the children depending on their stage of development. For very young children, they can make any shape they wish. They must stay 'frozen' in this shape until the music starts again. If they move they have to sit down. The winner is the last child standing.

3. Model some shapes for them to copy.

And another idea:

▶ Encourage the children to draw the shapes and describe them.

▶ Encourage the children's input, ideas for different shapes, types of music, etc.

▶ Chalk some very large shape outlines on the ground and when the music stops, the children have to run into a shape outline and make their bodies into that shape!

Beach hunt

These are ideal adult-led activities for between 4-6 children.

Ideas for focus:

▶ How many objects can you find?

▶ Can you find a specific number of certain types of object?

What you need:

▶ large heavy duty plastic sheeting

▶ several bags of play sand or washed river sand

▶ community play blocks, large pebbles or boulders

▶ metal detectors

▶ sieves and/or fishing nets

▶ a range of large sand moulds

▶ a range of large spoons, a variety of plastic jugs, cups, etc

▶ a variety of objects such as plastic fish, rubber snakes, plastic coins, plastic numbers etc

▶ an outdoor water tap or water barrel

▶ metal washers or magnetic strips to fasten to non-magnetic objects

▶ a child-friendly digital camera

Key mathematical language:

number names, how many, most, least, set, large, small, pieces, half, third, quarter

---

Before you start:

▶ Create a large attractive outdoor 'beach' in a suitably accessible space, arranging the sand on the heavy duty sheeting. Or use your existing sand pit.

▶ Create an edging to your beach with the community play blocks, large pebbles, boulders or other suitable alternatives. Add water (using jugs) as appropriate to the activity.

▶ Add the range of resources relevant to the beach or provide in smaller boxes within or to the side of the beach.

What you do:

1. Model the range of different activities the children could choose in this setting. These could include:

   ▷ using the metal detectors to find numbers buried in the sand and then making them into an ordered number line;

   ▷ using a simple drawn map to hunt for specific objects buried in the sand, and then sorting into sets all the similar objects e.g. all fish, snakes, etc and counting how many are in each set. The sorting of the objects can be supported by using small plastic hula hoops. For older children, they could be asked not to dig up certain objects and so will therefore have to dig carefully and perhaps incur a penalty if they dig up a wrong object?

   ▷ using sieves or small fishing nets to fish out plastic fish floating in the water and then counting to see who has caught the most or the least fish;

   ▷ using a range of moulds to make 'sand pies', then comparing size, quantity and shape;

   ▷ making an enormous cake in the sand using the spoons, cups etc and then cutting the cake into two, three, four pieces (halves, thirds, quarters).

Whichever activity you are doing, explain the rules repeatedly as required.

And another idea:

▶ Encourage the children to decide on the activity and the resources needed as well as how the hunt will be organised and what the rules are.

▶ Use a digital camera to capture aspects of the hunt and support children's mark making or writing about the activity.

Bottles on the wall

This is an ideal activity for working in small groups.

Ideas for focus:

▶ To use hand-eye coordination to throw a beanbag and knock over objects

▶ To predict distance and speed

▶ To work out your score by adding the numbers on the bottles

What you need:

▶ (1 litre) recycled plastic bottles

▶ paper/card number labels and sticking tape

▶ a variety of coloured beanbags – 3 of each colour

▶ a box, table or low wall (to stand the bottles on)

▶ an outdoor number line

▶ access to water from a water butt or outside tap

▶ jumbo chalk

▶ a chalkboard

Key mathematical language:

number names, addition, more than, less than, first, second, third, highest

Before you start:

▶ Stick number labels onto the plastic bottles.

▶ Set up the bottles on a suitably raised surface e.g. a box, low wall or table. Set them far enough apart to challenge the stage of development of the children.

▶ Draw a chalk start line for players to stand behind for throwing.

▶ Provide beanbags in a box or bucket for children to pick three beanbags of the same colour.

What you do:

1. Each child has three turns to throw a beanbag from behind the start line, and knock down a plastic bottle. For very young children, the winner could be the one who has knocked down the most bottles. For older children, they score the number that is on that bottle they knocked down and the winner is the child with the highest score.

2. Demonstrate the game. Explain that the winner can be decided in two ways i.e. who knocks down the most bottles or who has the highest based on the total of numbers on the bottles.

3. For adding up the scores, model using the number line to add the numbers together using marker pegs to visualise the counting on. Suggest strategies to use such as starting with the highest number and counting on from this.

4. Explain the rules repeatedly as required.

And another idea:

▶ Help the children to start the activity and then leave them to play independently – with any adult support only provided at intervals.

▶ Encourage the children to decide co-operatively on their own rules.

Can the cans

This is an extended activity to 'Bottles on the wall'. It is more difficult due to the smaller size and weight of the cans.

Ideas for focus:

▶ To problem solve how to cause the largest number of cans to fall off the wall

▶ To add the scores on the cans to find out who has the highest score

What you need:

▶ a set of 12 or more purpose made plastic cans (available from pound shops or early years suppliers) or empty fizzy drink cans with the ring pulls removed and holes taped over

▶ a variety of coloured beanbags – 3 of each colour

▶ laminated numbers pegged onto a string to make a number line

▶ paper/card number labels and sticking tape

▶ a chalkboard

▶ a large cardboard box

▶ chalk

Key mathematical language:

how many?, number names 0–10 and beyond, more than, less than

Before you start:

▶ Label each of the cans with a number using the paper/card and sticking tape.

▶ Choose how many cans you want to use and stack the cans in the required formation, e.g. stacked on top of each other in a specific formation 5, 4, 3, 2, 1, or in a line, on the large cardboard box.

▶ Draw a chalk line for players to stand behind and throw from.

▶ Provide beanbags in a box/bucket for children to choose 3 of the same colour.

▶ Set up the pegged number line and 'scoreboard'/chalkboard close by.

What you do:

1. Model the activity by explaining that the winner can be decided in a number of ways e.g. who knocks down the most cans or who has the highest score when the numbers on the cans are added together at the end.

2. For adding up the scores, model using the number line to add the numbers together. Use marker pegs to visualise the counting on and suggest strategies to use such as starting with the highest number and counting on from this.

And another idea:

▶ Help the children to start the activity and then leave them to play independently with any adult support only provided at intervals.

▶ Make the resources available in the continuous outdoor provision. Encourage the children to set up and play the game independently including chalking the lines, etc.

▶ With more able children ask them to write tips on how to win the 'can the cans' game.

Shape hunt

Use as a focused adult-led activity for 4-6 children working in pairs.

Ideas for focus:

▶ To listen to positional clues to find the laminated shape pictures

▶ To work co-operatively in pairs to find the shapes within a set time

What you need:

▶ A4 laminated cards depicting 2D and 3D shapes

▶ laminated cards with 4 smaller versions of a selection of the 2D and 3D shapes

▶ 2 or 3 minute sand or wind-up timer

▶ talking tins or an audio tape recorder (to record positional clues)

▶ an attractively decorated box

Key mathematical language:

2D and 3D shape names, under, over, behind, next to, on top of, in front of

Before you start:

▶ Record your positional clues using the audio equipment. Examples of audio clues: 'The square is hanging under the tree', 'The cube is on top of the tree house', 'The circle is under the bench'.

▶ Hang or place the laminated shape cards outdoors according to the positional audio clues.

▶ Place the cards with the 4 smaller images into the box for children to select from.

What you do:

1. Explain that the task is to find the 4 different shapes on the laminated cards before the sand timer runs out.

2. Play the audio positional clues for the children to listen to. Encourage them to listen carefully and talk to each other in their pairs.

3. Ask the children to choose a card from the box.

4. Set the timer when the children are ready to start to hunt and collect the shape images!

And another idea:

▶ Ask 2 of the children to decide where to hide the laminated cards. They can even record the positional clues themselves and then hang or place the laminated images appropriately.

Blowing bubbles

Ideas for focus:

▶ To blow bubbles, observe them and describe where they go/what they do

What you need:

▶ bubble pots of different sizes

▶ a child-friendly digital camera

I will need

Key mathematical language:

over, under, above, between, higher, lower, big, small, medium, light

Before you start:

▶ Set up a range of bubble pots in a suitable location in the outdoor setting.

What you do:

1. Show the children the bubble tubs and demonstrate how to blow bubbles.

2. Explain to the children that they are going to blow bubbles and then watch very carefully where they go!

3. Let the children blow the bubbles and watch closely where the bubbles go and what they do. Some of the children who are not blowing the bubbles can take photographs.

4. Encourage the children to talk about what direction and where the bubbles go.

And another idea:

▶ Use the photographs of the bubbles to make a picture book.

▶ Encourage the children to write about their experience of blowing bubbles and write descriptions of where the bubbles went.

Fill the bucket

This is an ideal adult-led activity for a group of four children working in pairs.

What you need:

- ▶ 2 large buckets
- ▶ 2 long lengths of 25mm clear plastic piping (each 6–8 ft long)
- ▶ 2 large funnels
- ▶ jugs (different sizes and shapes)
- ▶ an outdoor water butt
- ▶ plastic steps

Key mathematical language:

large, small, medium, faster, slower, full to the brim

Before you start:

▶ Fix the two funnels to one end of each of the two pipes, then attach to the fence at the same height.

▶ Place a bucket under the open end of each pipe, ensuring that the two pipes and buckets are fixed at exactly the same height.

▶ Place a water butt full of water in between the two pipes and buckets.

▶ If necessary, provide steps for the children to access the funnels.

What you do:

1. Explain to the children that the task is to fill the bucket right to the top as quickly as possible, by pouring water into the funnel using a jug of their choice.

2. Line the children up into two teams.

3. Each child takes a turn to fill the jug from the water butt and pour it into the funnel.

4. The winning team is the team whose bucket is full to the brim first.

4. Show the children how to tally how many jugs it takes to fill the bucket.

And another idea:

▶ Challenge the children to problem solve using different sized jugs or jugs with only one or two small holes in them.

▶ Place larger buckets at the end of the pipes.

▶ Use sand timers to challenge the children to fill the bucket in less than three minutes.

Do the course

This is an ideal adult-led activity for a group of four children working individually.

Ideas for focus:

▶ To play a game in order from designated starting points

▶ To tally and add up the number of shots taken

What you need:

▶ a medium-sized flat grassy space

▶ child-sized mini putting clubs and balls

▶ mini flags – made from laminated paper with numbers (1–9) written on them fastened to the top of canes

▶ 60 mm (approx) circular holes made in the grass or, alternatively, margarine tubs with one side cut out and fastened to the ground with short metal pegs

▶ laminated A5 cards with the hole number and 'start' written on (e.g. 'START HOLE 1') fastened to the ground with a short metal peg

---

Key mathematical language:

how many, number names and number order, more than, less than, most, least, the difference

---

Before you start:

▶ Work together with the children to create the mini flags numbered from 1–9 (depending on the number of holes of the course).

▶ Create your mini-golf course of 'holes' using circular cut outs in the grass, or fastened down margarine tubs.

▶ Fix the starting signs for each hole by sticking pegs into the ground.

What you do:

1. Show the children how to hold the club. Demonstrate how you hit the ball safely.

2. Explain to the children the rules of the game and how to play safely. They must try to use the club to send or 'putt' the ball into each numbered hole in the least number of shots. Starting at 1, they then move on to 2, then 3 and so on to complete the course. Tell the children they can only touch the ball with the club and must make sure that no one is standing close to them when they take their shot.

3. Explain how to score and how to tally the number of shots taken to put the ball into the hole from the start position.

4. Play a round!

5. Once the children understand the scoring system, ask them, 'How many shots does it take to complete the hole?' Then, help them to add up the total number of shots it takes them to complete the course (or part of the course).

6. Children can be encouraged to see who has taken the most or the least shots and what the difference is.

And another idea:

▶ Develop the use of mini scoring cards that the children can individually complete by tallying each time they take a shot and then adding these marks up at the end of each hole.

▶ Help children to write a set of course rules e.g. don't lift your club higher than your knee, wait until the person in front has finished the hole before starting it yourself.

▶ Shuffle the number cards and play the course in that order (e.g. 2, 5, 4, 7, 8, 1, 2, 9, 3, 6 instead of 1, 2, 3, 4, 5, 6, 7, 8, 9).

redict ball games

Ideal activity for small groups of 2-6 children.

Ideas for focus:

▶ To set and complete challenges

What you need:

▶ sand or wind-up timers

▶ variety of sizes of balls (small/medium/large)

▶ plastic hoops

▶ a large wall board and marker pens

▶ sets of 'challenge cards'

Key mathematical language

how many, number names, more than, less than, most, least, positional language, through, into

---

Before you start:

▶ Make the 'challenge cards' (the instructions for the different challenges) that you would like the children to try. Set the challenges, and the challenge cards, as appropriate to the stage of development of the children e.g. draw a description of the challenge rather than write it.

▶ Set up all the resources in an appropriate area – where children can play without being disturbed by other activities.

▶ Ensure the wall board and writing implements are readily available.

What you do:

1. Gather the children together and show them the challenge cards. Tell them that, working in pairs, they are going to pick and carefully read a challenge card, and take on that timed ball game challenge! Each of the challenges involves how many times or how fast they can do the activity.

2. Ask the children to predict how many times they think they can e.g. throw and catch the ball in one minute. Explain to the children that 'predict' means to make an informed guess, before they start an activity, as to how many times they can do something in a specific time e.g. roll a ball backwards and forwards to a partner in one minute.

3. Demonstrate how to tally how many times they manage to do something.

4. Model the use of the resources and show the children how to record the results of a challenge on the large boards.

   Here are some ball games to start you off:

   ▷ Rolling a ball to a partner as many times as possible in one minute with another child tallying each roll. Tally marks are added up at the end to see how many times the ball was rolled. Repeat the activity, this time trying to beat the previous score.

   ▷ Throwing a ball to a partner as many times as possible in two minutes, again with another person tallying each throw and then totalling up the number of throws at the end of two minutes.

   ▷ Throwing a ball in the air and catching it as many times as possible without dropping it, in one minute. In pairs, one child should throw and catch the ball with the other child tallying and counting how many times they manage it. Then the children swap places.

   ▷ Bouncing a ball inside a plastic hoop as many times as possible in one minute.

5. For all the activities use the sand or wind-up timer.

And another idea:

▶ Add up all the scores and see who has the highest score. Ask the children how many is **one more** than the number they have scored and **one less** than the number they have scored.

▶ Ask the children to make up their own ball game challenge. Ask them to write their own challenge on a challenge card.

Knock them down

Ideas for focus:

▶ To knock over as many skittles as you can

▶ To add up and record scores

What you need:

▶ a set of skittles (quarter fill large lemonade or water bottles with water, seal the tops with sellotape and stick numbered cards to the front of the bottles)

▶ a variety of different sizes and types of ball

▶ a set of pictures showing how the skittles can be set up in different formations e.g. triangle, square, rectangle, circle

▶ jumbo chalk and marker pens

▶ an outdoor number line

Key mathematical language:

how many, number names, more than, less than, most, least, positional language, through, into

Before you start:

▶ Mark out a skittle/bowling alley with the chalk on an appropriate, flat outdoor surface.

▶ Number each of the skittles with the number it is worth e.g. 1, 2, 3. Then, set up the skittles in a specific formation e.g. a triangle.

▶ Provide a variety of different balls for children to choose from in an accessible trug or large box.

What you do:

1. Explain to the children the aim of the activity, i.e. to take turns to knock down as many skittles as possible. Demonstrate the technique of rolling the ball down the alley (some of the children may be familiar with this game from going ten pin bowling with their families).

2. Show the children how to record the scores. You can choose to either count up the number of skittles or the numbers on them.

3. Encourage the children to take it in turns to aim at the skittles and knock as many down as they can. Use the outdoor number line to help with the calculations and then record them on the scoreboard.

4. Now, set up a different formation of the skittles, e.g. a circle, and play again.

And another idea:

▶ Create a permanent skittle alley in the setting e.g. use large wooden sleeper type materials to create the sides and back of the alley. Provide linked permanent resources for recording the scores.

▶ Encourage the children to come up with some new or extra rules of their own and write them down.

▶ Children at a higher stage of development (Reception) could play this game in teams.

Build it!

Ideas for focus:

▶ To problem solve how to use materials to build a stable den structure

▶ To build a den to a specific criteria e.g. long and thin or suitable for 6 children to fit in, etc.

What you need:

A range and variety of den making materials including some of the following:

▶ several large cardboard tubes

▶ a range of different sized cardboard boxes – flattened out

▶ heavy drapes such as old curtains or heavy duty plastic sheeting

▶ sheets of tarpaulin

▶ old bed sheets and blankets

▶ different sized clothes pegs

▶ a selection of different sized bamboo canes (available from garden centres)

▶ thin ropes

▶ velcro

▶ masking tape, grey gaffer tape and scissors

Key mathematical language:

big, small, medium, long/longer, short/shorter, thick/thin, high/low, cylindrical

Before you start:

▶ Collect and set out the range of resources in an easily accessible and safe way within a suitably large space.

What you do:

1. Show the range of resources to the children and tell them that you are going to build a den together! Ask them what they would like their den to look like. Discuss ideas together as a group.

2. Work with the children to discuss their ideas and model how to safely use some of the resources – including use of fastenings like gaffer tape, pegs and velcro.

3. Talk with the children about how to keep safe and what this means in terms of using the resource and materials.

4. After discussing the children's ideas, help them to put these into place.

5. Once the den is finished, let the children go inside and enjoy sitting in their den!

And another idea:

▶ Encourage the children to try out new ideas and ways of building. Look at pictures of dens in books or online.

▶ Take photographs of your finished den and make a book, encouraging the children to write stage appropriate captions and descriptions (or an adult can scribe for the children).

Hanging out the washing

Work with groups of 3-6 children.

Ideas for focus:

▶ To problem solve how to order clothes items in (i) order of size, (ii) groups of the same thing e.g. socks, (iii) sequence of putting items on when dressing, (iv) order of quantities e.g. 1 shoe, 2 hats, 3 coats, 4 scarves etc

What you need:

▶ washing lines and clothes pegs

▶ a range and variety of baby or doll's clothes

▶ a laminated set of pictures of clothing items 1–20 (e.g. 1 sock, 2 shoes, 3 scarves, 4 hats, etc.)

▶ a digital camera

Key mathematical language:

big/bigger, small/smaller, large/larger, medium, number names

Before you start:

▶ Set up the range of resources in an easily accessible and safe way within a suitably large space. Provide clothes pegs in a small basket or bowl.

▶ Securely fix the washing line in a safe position and at a height where children can easily reach it.

What you do:

1. Demonstrate and model creating a range of patterns using the clothes and pegs on the washing line.

2. Help the children to hang out the washing, creating recurring patterns using the clothes e.g. one sock, two vests, one sock, two vests, one sock, two vests and so on.

3. Now do the same with the laminated images of the clothes in number order e.g. one hat, two socks, one hat, two socks and so on.

And another idea:

▶ Encourage the children to try out new ideas for creating different patterns.

▶ Encourage the children to take photographs of the patterns they have created using the digital camera and then to make a book of patterns they have made.

▶ Leave the washing line hanging up and provide the resources (the clothes and/or the laminated pictures) as part of the continuous provision range outdoors for children to use independently.

Net the duck

Ideas for focus:

▶ To create a number line using the numbers on the ducks

What you need:

▶ a range of small plastic ducks with numbers written in permanent marker on the undersides

▶ child-sized fishing nets

▶ a large builder's tray or suitable alternative

▶ an outdoor number line

Key mathematical language:

number names, number order, one more than, one less than

Before you start:

▶ Set the tray on the floor in a suitable outdoor space. Fill it with shallow water.

▶ Use a marker pen to write numbers on the undersides of the plastic ducks. Put the numbered ducks in the water.

▶ Put the outdoor number line alongside the tray.

What you do:

1. Work with the children to model the activity of fishing a duck from the 'pond' with the fishing net and placing it on the number line on the floor according to the number marked on its underside.

2. Model how to engage safely with the activity. Talk about the dangers of water (even shallow water) and how to be careful with the fishing nets – keep the poles away from eyes.

3. Challenge the children to try to complete a number line of ducks.

And another idea:

▶ This activity can be differentiated, starting from a number line up to 5 to a much larger one of 20 or more!

▶ Provide the resources for children to engage with independently as part of the setting's continuous outdoor provision.

Ball in play

Ideas for focus:

▶ To add the total of points scored as the ball is sent through a number of hoops

▶ To send a ball through a number of hoops to achieve a predetermined number

What you need:

▶ child-sized croquet type mallets, balls

▶ wire hoops

▶ a start/finish peg

▶ an outdoor number line

▶ a marker board and marker pens

▶ card and sellotape (to affix the numbers to the hoops)

Key mathematical language:

how many, number names, more than, less than

Before you start:

▶ Set up a croquet course on appropriate ground i.e. grass, packed mud or sand.

▶ Hammer in the hoops and the start/finish peg.

▶ Attach numbers up to 5, 10 or 20 to the tops of the hoops.

▶ Supply the child-sized croquet mallets and balls in a bucket or box close by.

What you do:

1. Demonstrate and then help the children to correctly and safely use the croquet mallet and ball.

2. Model how to 'send' the ball through the hoop in number order 1-5, 1-10 or 1-20.

3. Explain that the ball must pass under the hoop to count. Give the children time to practise sending the ball through a hoop. Children play individually to begin with (children of a higher developmental stage could be organized into playing in pairs or teams).

4. Explain and demonstrate how the scoring works: they score the number on the hoop that the ball has gone through.

And another idea:

▶ Once the children have become confident with this game, extend their learning by helping them to 'send' the ball through a number of hoops to make a 'total' number, e.g. if the total number is 9, the ball will have to have been sent through 3 hoops totalling 9 to win e.g. hoops 3, 5 and 1 or 2, 3, 4. Appropriate use of the number line can greatly help children to understand the concept of this.

Money grabber

Ideal for groups of four children (2 pairs).

Ideas for focus:

▶ To listen to instructions and use hand-eye coordination to fish out items from a water tray

What you need:

▶ 2 similar sized water trays

▶ a sand or wind-up timer

▶ an eye mask (soft elasticated material)

▶ up to 10 small waterproof sacks of 1p, 2p, 5p, 10p coins (of varying amounts and denominations)

▶ 2 child-sized litter pickers/grabbers

Key mathematical language:

names of coins, next to, forwards, backwards, left, right, a bit, a lot

Before you start:

▶ Set up the resources in a suitable outdoor space.

▶ Make up the mini sacks of coins – ready to place into the water trays once the eye masks are in place!

▶ Show the children the litter pickers and ask them what they think they are for. Model the use of the litter pickers and let the children try them out.

What you do:

1. Two pairs of children will compete to see which pair can fish out the greatest number of coin sacks (and therefore the most money!) from the trays in the time given. One child is blindfolded and must find and fish out the coin sacks with the litter picker – using the other child's directions to where they need to move their picker!

2. Once a child from each pair has the eye mask in place then the practitioner places the coin bags into the trays (in similar places in both trays) and gives the blindfolded child a litter picker. Place the sacks with the largest amount of coins closer to the sides of the water tray where they are more difficult to 'grab'.

3. Set two or three minutes on the timer and then call 'Start!'

4. The partner then gives the blindfolded child verbal instruction to help them to pick up as many of the mini coin sacks as possible before the time runs out.

5. Once the time is up, the sacks collected are emptied and the coins counted. The winning team is the one with the most money fished out!

6. The children then swap roles and play again.

And another idea:

▶ Encourage the children to try out new ideas/ways of playing the activity by changing the amount of time or the rules.

▶ Discuss with the children the best strategies to use and encourage them to write down their top tips to share with other children.

Personalised number plates

Ideas for focus:

▶ To write numbers and letters

What you need:

▶ lots of blank pieces of card in the shape and size of vehicle number plates

▶ some examples of old number plates

▶ felt tip pens

▶ number fans (0–5 or 0–9)

▶ letter fans (as appropriate)

▶ wheeled toys

▶ string or tape (to fasten the number plates to the wheeled toys)

▶ an outdoor number line

Key mathematical language:

Front, back, number names, next to, in front of

Before you start:

▶ Set out the resources in a suitable area of your outdoor setting and display photos of vehicles with number plates (from books, magazines and the internet). If possible have some real number plates on display.

What you do:

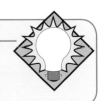

1. Show the children the old number plates (real or photographs).

2. Work with the children to create their own personalized number plates. Explain why they will need two plates which are the same – one for the front and one for the back of the vehicle.

3. Use the number and letter fans and the number line to support children's visualisation of the number shapes.

4. Help the children to fix their number plates to the wheeled toys.

And another idea:

▶ Ask children to find out what the number plate is on their family car.

Steps to the target

Ideas for focus:

▶ To throw bean bags accurately within a target area

What you need:

▶ jumbo chalk

▶ a teddy bear or other soft toy

▶ a range of beanbags – two of each colour

▶ a large rubber or foam dice

▶ an outdoor number line

▶ a board (to record results)

Key mathematical language:

number names, colour names, add together, total, near, closer

Before you start:

▶ Chalk a circle target on a hard surface, approximately 1.5m diameter with an inner circle of approximately 0.5m.

▶ Mark a start line about 3m from the edge of the circle.

▶ Place the teddy in the centre of the inner circle.

▶ Supply the beanbags in a bucket for children to access easily.

What you do:

1. Explain that the purpose of the activity is to land the whole beanbag in the target area – either in the inner circle (next to the teddy) or outer circle. The aim of the game is to gently hit the teddy with the beanbag for maximum points.

2. Explain how the scoring works: 5 points if the beanbag lands in the inner circle, 1 point if it lands in the outer circle, 2 bonus points if the bean bag is touching the teddy in the inner circle. An adult acts as judge for borderline cases – deciding whether the bean bag is inside the inner circle or not.

3. Each child has two turns and their scores are recorded on a board (by an adult). Their two scores are then added together to make their final total. The highest score is declared the winner.

And another idea:

▶ To make the activity more challenging, each child could roll a big dice before they throw their beanbags and take a tiny step forward for every number thrown on the dice e.g. if the child rolls a 3, they take three tiny steps forward. Or you could have a rule that if odd numbers (1, 3, 5) are rolled they must take a tiny step backwards, and for even numbers (2, 4, 6) a step forward.

In the trug

This is a game for pairs of children to work together co-operatively.

Ideas for focus:

▶ To land as many beanbags in the trug within the time allowed

What you need:

▶ 3 different coloured trugs

▶ three sets of 10 beanbags (each set to be a different colour)

▶ jumbo chalk

▶ an outdoor number line

▶ a board (to record scores)

▶ a sand or wind-up timer

Key mathematical language:

how many, number names, more, less

Before you start:

▶ Mark two chalk lines on a suitable hard surface – a line along which the trugs will be placed and another line from behind which the children will throw the beanbags into the trugs.

What you do:

1. Each pair has 5 beanbags each of the same colour and takes it in turns to throw a beanbag so it lands in a trug.

2. Rules of the game:

   ▷ A limited time is set of 1–2 minutes

   ▷ Beanbags that miss cannot be reused/rethrown

   ▷ Once the time is up no further beanbags are to be thrown and the beanbags in each trug are counted.

3. Results are chalked onto the scoreboard. Then the pairs have another turn and the scores are again recorded. The two scores from each set of throws are added together to find the winning pair.

And another idea:

▶ The game can be differentiated by moving the throwing line further away from the trugs.

Climb the ladder

Ideas for focus:

▶ To get to the top of the ladder in the least number of turns of throwing the dice

What you need:

▶ jumbo chalk

▶ a large jumbo dice

▶ a board (to record scores)

Key mathematical language:

number names, add together, more

Before you start:

▶ Mark two appropriately sized chalk ladders in parallel onto a hard surface area of your outdoor setting.

▶ Number the spaces between the rungs from 0–5, 10–20.

What you do:

1. Explain to the children that this is a game between two children or two pairs of children. Model how the game works. Explain that the winner is the one who gets to the top of the ladder first.

2. Each player rolls the dice – the person with the highest number goes first. Then each team takes it in turn to roll the dice and move from the 0 upwards – marking their current place on the ladder using a beanbag.

3. The team who reaches the top number in the ladder first is the winner.

And another idea:

▶ Encourage the children to alter the existing rules or create their own rules.

▶ The size of the ladders and the numbers on the dice can be differentiated e.g. just 1, 2, 3 on the dice faces or a ladder of 5, 10 or 20 spaces.

Fish it out

Ideas for focus:

▶ To fish out numbered balls and identify them

▶ To make larger numbers by adding the numbers on the balls together

What you need:

▶ 5–20 small plastic balls

▶ child-sized fishing nets

▶ a water trough or builder's tray

▶ a black or blue permanent marker pen

▶ an outdoor number line

▶ a board (to record scores)

Key mathematical language:

number names, more than, less than, add together

Before you start:

▶ Mark the balls with a number between 1–10. There may be more than one of each number.

▶ Set the water tray on the floor in a suitable outdoor space, fill it with water and put the balls in.

▶ Set out the fishing nets and scoreboard.

What you do:

1. Allow the children to practise fishing out the balls using the nets, and calling out the numbers on them.

2. Explain to the children that the purpose of the activity is to fish out two balls and add together the two numbers on them to get a total score.

3. Model fishing out two balls and adding together the two numbers using the number line.

4. Record the number on the board.

5. Start the game!

And another idea:

▶ Ask the children to try fishing out three balls and adding the numbers together.

Reach for the stars

Ideas for focus:

▶ To climb the ladder the quickest and then be the first to cover all three stars!

What you need:

▶ jumbo chalk

▶ a large foam or rubber dice

▶ coloured beanbags (5 sets of 2 colours)

▶ an outdoor number line

Key mathematical language:

number names, more than, colour names

Before you start:

▶ Chalk two parallel ladders up to 0–10 or 0–20 onto the hard surfacing area of your outdoor area. Chalk the word 'START' at the bottom of each ladder. Just above the ladder chalk three stars.

▶ Set out the dice and beanbags.

What you do:

1. Arrange the children into two pairs.

2. Explain that the goal is to climb to the top of the ladder and cover each star with a beanbag by reaching the top of the ladder first three times.

3. Each pair throws the dice to decide who goes first with the lowest number thrown going first.

4. Each pair takes it in turns to roll the dice and move the beanbag up the wrungs of the ladder the number of spots on the dice. Once a pair reaches the top they place a beanbag over a star. The losing team then goes first in the next round.

5. The first pair to reach the top of the ladder and cover all three stars is the winning pair!

6. It is a good idea to leave a beanbag where the pair is at and then mark the new position (when the dice has been rolled) with another beanbag. This allows a visual check to be made that the correct number of steps (wrungs) have been correctly moved up e.g. 4.

And another idea:

▶ Encourage children to change the rules and/or make up their own rules for this game.

Listen and find

Ideas for focus:

▶ To listen to the clues and find the toys hidden in the given time

What you need:

▶ a range of large toys (up to 10 or 20) with which the children are familiar e.g. a favourite teddy bear, action figure, doll, animation character etc.

▶ talking tins with recorded clues on e.g. 'Teddy is under the wheelbarrow' or alternatively, tape recorded messages

▶ pictures or photographs of the toys on laminated sheets

▶ a wind-up or sand timer

Key mathematical language:

next to, underneath, on top of, close to, behind, in front of

Before you start:

▶ Pre-record the clues of where the toys are hidden in your outdoor area using positional language such as over, under, behind, in front of, etc.

▶ Place the laminated images of the toys alongside the recorded clues so that it is clear which clue refers to which toy.

What you do:

1. Explain to the children that the idea is to work in pairs to find as many of the toys as possible in a specified time e.g. 1, 2 or 3 minutes.

2. Model listening to the clue, then going to try to find the toy. Explain that once they have found the toy the children should circle the picture on the laminated sheet with the marker pen and then listen to the next clue and go off to find the toy in the clue.

3. Remind the children that they are to leave the toys where they find them as others will also be using the same clues.

4. Try this activity with just two pairs of children initially, then extend the activity to involve a larger group.

And another idea:

▶ Allow the children to record clues and help to hide the toys.

Measure it

Ideal activity for 3-6 children.

Ideas for focus:

▶ To use non standard units to measure

What you need:

▶ jumbo chalk

▶ a child-friendly digital camera

▶ an outdoor number line

Key mathematical language:

how many, number names, hand span, stride, foot span, steps, longer, shorter

Before you start:

▶ Gather the children all together and explain what the activity involves.

What you do:

1. Explain to the children how they can measure the length of their body or part of their body e.g. an arm or leg.

2. Introduce the idea of using strides or hand spans or other non standard measures e.g. foot span.

3. Model drawing round the body of a willing volunteer and then let the children draw round you.

4. Try measuring using strides, hand spans, steps and foot spans. Ask the children which they think is best/easiest/most accurate.

And another idea:

▶ Ask the children to measure other things that they find in the outdoor space of your setting e.g. the length of an outdoor bench or a flowerbed etc.

▶ Make a book with the children of things they have measured and either scribe for the children or encourage them to write their own measurements with captions and comments.

The **Little Books** series consists of:

All Through the Year
Bags, Boxes & Trays
Bricks and Boxes
Celebrations
Christmas
Circle Time
Clay and Malleable
Materials
Clothes and Fabrics
Colour, Shape and Number
Cooking from Stories
Cooking Together
Counting
Dance
Dance, with music CD
Discovery Bottles
Dough
50
Fine Motor Skills
Fun on a Shoestring
Games with Sounds
Growing Things
ICT
Investigations
Junk Music
Language Fun
Light and Shadow

Listening
Living Things
Look and Listen
Making Books and Cards
Making Poetry
Mark Making
Maths Activities
Maths from Stories
Maths Songs and Games
Messy Play
Music
Nursery Rhymes
Outdoor Play
Outside in All Weathers
Parachute Play
Persona Dolls
Phonics
Playground Games
Prop Boxes for Role Play
Props for Writing
Puppet Making
Puppets in Stories
Resistant Materials
Role Play
Sand and Water
Science through Art
Scissor Skills

Sewing and Weaving
Small World Play
Sound Ideas
Storyboards
Storytelling
Seasons
Time and Money
Time and Place
Treasure Baskets
Treasureboxes
Tuff Spot Activities
Washing Lines
Writing

All available from
www.acblack.com/featherstone